Little Mitchie

DANGEROUS NATURE

WEIRD, WILD, AND WONDERFUL

TAMRA B. ORR

CREATING YOUNG NONFICTION READERS

Little Mitchie books spark curiosity and support early nonfiction reading for students in Grades 2-3. Designed to build vocabulary, support second language learners, and prepare readers for middle-grade content, each book includes helpful tips for parents and educators to build confidence and deepen understanding of the world.

TIPS FOR READING NONFICTION WITH BEGINNING READERS

Talk about Nonfiction

Begin by explaining that nonfiction books give us information that is true. The book will be organized around a specific topic or idea, and we may learn new facts through reading.

Look at the Parts

Most nonfiction books have helpful features. Our *Little Mitchie* titles include color photographs and graphic aids, a table of contents, a glossary, and an index. Share the purpose of these features with your reader.

Color Photos and Graphic Aids

A lot of information can be found by "reading" photos, charts, maps, and other graphic aids found within nonfiction texts. Help your reader learn more about the different ways information can be displayed.

Table of Contents

Located at the front of the book, this list shows the big ideas within the text and the page numbers where they can be found.

Glossary

Located at the back of the book, the glossary defines key words and phrases that are related to the topic. These words and phrases can be found in the text in colored type.

Index

Located at the back of the book, an index is an alphabetical list of topics and the page numbers where they can be found.

With a little help and guidance about reading nonfiction, you can feel good about introducing a young reader to the world of *Little Mitchie* nonfiction books.

Little Mitchie is an imprint of:

Mitchell Lane
PUBLISHERS

2001 SW 31st Avenue
Hallandale, FL 33009
mitchelllanepub.com

First Edition, 2027.

Author: Tamra B. Orr
Designer: Jen Bowers
Editor: Tricia Hoffman
Library of Congress Cataloging-in-Publication Data
Title: Dangerous Nature / by Tamra Orr

Description: Hallandale, FL :
Mitchell Lane Publishers, [2027]

Identifiers:
ISBN 979-8-89260-891-6 (library bound)
ISBN 979-8-89260-994-4 (eBook)

Library of Congress Control Number: 2026936368

PHOTO CREDITS
Shutterstock: cover, p.1, p.22 ©2017 nechaevkon, p.5 ©2024 Gallwis, p.7 ©2020 Piu_Piu, p.8 ©2017 tome213, p.9 ©2010 Gary Whitton, p.10 ©2025 FX Budijanto Sundjaja, p.11 ©2024 lordnore, p.12 ©2023 caioacquesta, p.13 ©2016 Sergey Uryadnikov, p.14 ©2020 Dimitri Lisitsyn, p.16–17 ©2016 giannimarchetti, p.19 ©2018 Nickolas warner, p.20 ©2008 Liz Van Steenburgh, p.21 ©2014 Bildagentur Zoonar GmbH, p.22 ©2020 Kichigin, ©2016 Rodrigo Lourezini

TABLE OF CONTENTS

Chapter One

EXPLORE THE DANGER

Nature is beautiful. But it can also be dangerous! Get ready to explore extreme temperatures, scary creatures, and bizarre locations around the world.

BELOW THE WAVES

Deep down on the ocean floor are vents that look like underwater chimneys spilling black smoke. The water is more than 700 degrees Fahrenheit (371 degrees Celsius)! It is heated by the **magma** below.

Chapter Two

FROSTBITE AND FLAMES

A town nicknamed "The Pole of Cold" has to be chilly! The village of Oymyakon in Russia is the coldest place in the world where people live.

In winter, Oymyakon's temperatures dip way below zero! Average temperatures during the day are –50 degrees Fahrenheit (–45 degrees Celsius). The lowest temperature ever recorded there was in 1933. It dropped to –90 degrees Fahrenheit (–68 degrees Celsius)!

40
20
60
0
80
-20
100
-40
120
-60
°F
°F
°C
°C

Indonesia's Kawah Ijen volcano is very warm. But it is also dangerous! In its center is a crater filled with an acidic lake. It could kill a human in seconds! It releases gases that catch fire and make bright blue flames.

Chapter Three

SNAKES AND SKELETONS

Off the coast of Brazil is Snake Island. It looks beautiful, but don't be fooled. It is home to thousands of dangerous snakes! Golden lancehead snakes are some of the world's deadliest. Their **venom** kills prey almost instantly.

LAND DOWN UNDER

Australia is home to some deadly animals. Great white sharks, blue bottle jellyfish, funnel web spiders, and **taipans** all live there.

The Skeleton Coast in Namibia, Africa, is a scary place. It gets its name from the whale and seal bones that are scattered across the sand! The area is very dry and windy. It is part of one of the driest deserts in the world.

Along with the bones are the remains of ships and fishing boats. The Skeleton Coast is known for its thick fog, strong **currents**, and sharp rocks. More than a thousand ships have wrecked there.

Chapter Four

SALT AND SWALLOWS

Imagine a cave so deep that a 100-story building could fit inside! Visitors to Mexico's Cave of Swallows need very long ropes to reach the bottom. Inside the cave are thousands of birds that don't welcome guests.

PARACHUTE TIME

Some athletes go cave diving! They **freefall** into deep **vertical** caves. They might drop 2,000 feet (610 m) before opening a parachute.

WATCH THE WIND

Wind can be dangerous too. New Hampshire's Mount Washington has fierce winds. They once reached more than 230 miles (372 km) per hour. Climbing that mountain is dangerous!

Tanzania's Lake Natron is not for swimming! The water is **scalding** hot. Plus, it's filled with harsh salt and minerals that kill most creatures. It turns them into stone! What a weird, wild, and wonderful world we live in.

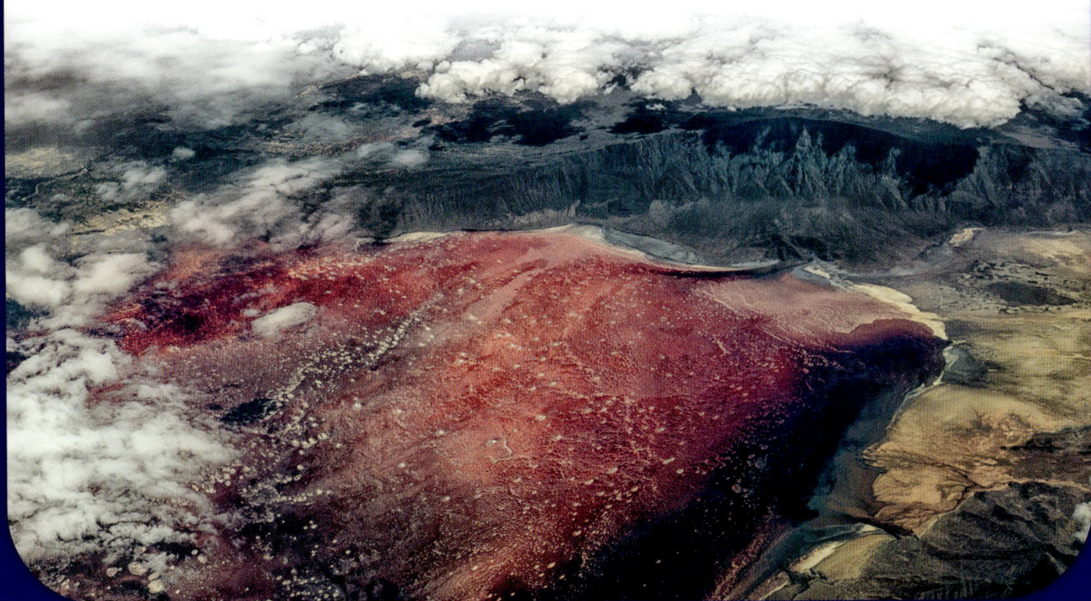

EVEN WILDER!

The mosquito is tiny. But it's actually the most dangerous creature in the world! It spreads diseases. Mosquitoes cause almost one million deaths per year!

The Bermuda Triangle in the Atlantic Ocean is a mystery. More than 50 ships and 20 planes have disappeared there!

The island of Vanuatu is in the South Pacific Ocean. It is always at risk of earthquakes, volcanic eruptions, and cyclones!

GLOSSARY

currents (kur-uhntz) the strong flow of water

freefall (free-fawl) the part of a jump before the opening of a parachute

frostbite (frawst-bite) a condition that occurs when extremely cold temperatures damage parts of a person's body

magma (mag-muh) melted rock found beneath Earth's surface that becomes lava when it flows out of volcanoes

scalding (skawl-ding) very hot liquid or steam that can burn

taipans (tye-panz) highly venomous snakes

venom (ven-uhm) the poisonous fluid snakes secrete when biting

vertical (vur-ti-kuhl) straight up and down

FURTHER READING

Birch, Greta. *Professor Hoot's Science Comics: Dangerous Animals.* Wayland, 2025.

O'Brien, Cynthia. *Cave Survival Stories.* Lerner Publications, 2025.

ON THE INTERNET

Ten Freaky Forces of Nature

https://kids.nationalgeographic.com/science/article/ten-freaky-forces-of-nature

Read about rogue waves, ball lightning, and more with National Geographic Kids.

Dangerous Facts for Kids

https://kids.kiddle.co/Dangerous

Learn more about dangerous animals, places, and activities—plus tips and tricks on staying safe!

INDEX